ISBN # Paperback 978-1-7380831-5-2
ISBN # E-book 978-1-7386735-8-2

Edited by **Dr. Rus**
Book Design by **Dr. Naqib Khan**
Published by **Warmina Foundation**

The book will be printed in Canada

Disclaimer:

The publisher and the authors do not make any guarantee or other promise as to any results that may be obtained from using the content of this book. This publication is meant as a source of valuable information for the reader, however it is not meant as a substitute for direct expert assistance. If such level of assistance is required, the services of a competent professional should be sought.

Table Of Contents

DEDICATION

This book is dedicated to all women, especially those utilizing their innate ability to nurture and care for others.

Today women are no longer bound by societal expectations or norms. Instead, they shatter glass ceilings becoming some of the most influential entrepreneurs.

I dedicate this book to all the women who fought to be treated like a woman should and didn't COMPROMISE!

"A Woman with A Voice Is By Definition A Strong Woman. But The Search To Find That Voice Can Be Remarkably Difficult."

-Melinda Gates

FOREWORD

For every successful man we usually find a circle of very successful women. This second installment of creative work by Warren Andrew Pinder is a testament to his commitment to inspire and share pearls of wisdom for another generation. It also reflects a level of focus and balanced approach for sharing both sides of the spectrum, for men and women alike.

Andrew boldly tackles what few men have done. Explore the disparities women face in Afro Centric Caribbean cultures with their male counterparts. While at the same time having the courage to live beyond it, with a chance at something more in their lives and their families. Holding nothing back in this round two of the series, as a professional colleague and young Bahamian woman who looks up to Andrew's leadership. I expect nothing less than a fearless conversation on how men are greatly influenced and made successful by the great and often unsung high-achieving pioneering women in their worlds. A great treat awaits in the pages up ahead.

Annie-Laurie Munroe

Ms. Domonique Bradford became a trusted friend of mine over thirty years ago. She was born and raised in Georgetown, Guyana, located in South America. After completing her secondary education, she served as a Police Officer at the Central Immigration and Passport Office. It was inspiring to watch her navigate the highs and lows of the work environment at such a young age while maintaining the utmost respect for herself and her colleagues. However, Ms. Bradford's vision of her future did not allow her to sit still. She migrated to Barbados and continued building a sound academic foundation. Then, having a strong desire for more, she moved to Canada, which has now become her home.

I was privileged to be one of her mentors during a portion of her adolescent years. From the tender age of ten, Ms. Bradford demonstrated wisdom, knowledge, and insight beyond her years. This, to some degree, is attributed to the mental and emotional strength she cultivated on her own without the robust support system the average teenager needs to accomplish their goals. As a result, she became one of the bravest young women I have ever encountered. She demonstrates the perfect mix of bravery, independence, humility, kindness, and strong moral values.

Without question, the years of focus, persistence, and self-motivation paid off. She became a mentor and a source of encouragement to many. I witnessed Ms. Bradford approached by individuals twice her age for advice on various topics, and it was truly amazing to watch. Did her strict morals cost her friendships over the years? Yes. Did that break her spirit? No. She remained her sweet, calm self, true to who she is.

It came as no surprise when she embarked on her second book, 'Achieve– Ma'am,' a fascinating and relevant topic. Women must read this book and engage in this discussion. You discover first and foremost, what you can achieve and how to accomplish your goals. Keep in mind men will also learn the art of guiding their partners toward achieving every goal they set for themselves.

'Achieve–Ma'am,' co-written by Ms. Domonique Bradford, a remarkable young woman who faced countless struggles, who fought endless battles, who endured, who survived, and who, beyond question, has achieved.

May God continue to bless and keep you, Domonique. I love whom you have become and I'm incredibly proud of your work.

Rhonda Eitokpah

INTRODUCTION

Time is an essential factor in life. Most lost opportunities are a result of not maximizing the time factor. Sometimes we find ourselves swamped and overwhelmed with activities. As a result, we don't have time for the most important things in life. Avoiding complacency ensures we are on time to crush our goals.

We have a tendency of doing things which take our time away from what's important for our growth. In order to grow and move forward we must identify what's important.

The motivation for this book came after publishing ACHIEVE-MEN. In that book, I encourage men to become confident, unleashing the power within to seek their God-given purpose. ACHIEVE-MEN is a tool for every man to use as motivation to align with fulfilling their goals and dreams.

In ACHIEVE-MA'AM, I will offer through the eyes of a son of a virtuous woman, and the grandson of two industrious grandmothers from both of my parents.

The content of this book includes information beneficial to females.

It includes 'What will a woman make happen.' Many times women are relegated to the background in our society. The good news is a number of women are breaking barriers and smashing the ceilings.

This book is set to correct a wrong mentality which believes a woman's life should end in the kitchen. It also sets out to correct the perception of women that they are merely a helpmate in very limited and traditional ways to their husbands.

History records women rising above societal ceilings and making a difference. They are super beings who refused to be relegated to the background. They shunned the mentality of being used as domestic enslaved people.

There's a need to correct the norm because something is wrong with the script. Women are beyond how society sometimes sees them. They are powerful instruments of change, and their aura oozes difference.

Some people see women as nothing more than baby factories. This is unjust to the female gender and demeaning.

This book addresses what a woman can do, the limits she's competent to break, the ceilings she knows how to break, and much more.

It explicitly discusses how a woman should build her intellectual capacity to compete favorably with her counterparts. While at the same time learning from examples of those who have once walked the path she is presently in.

The emphasis placed in this book is one of encouraging women to choose the role of a virtuous woman. As women, we should embrace the beauty of our youth as it radiates to other women around us.

By focusing on the above role and more, a woman prepares herself for the challenges of today's world. A world where she plays the role of a mother, father, sister, and breadwinner.

"The era where women used their bodies to achieve their goals has become extinct because they realized they are more than their bodies." The narrative has changed, and women are beginning to soar beyond society's expectations.

Chapter - 1

ACTION

What Should A Woman Make Happen?

ACTION:

What Should A Woman Make Happen?

Since the dawn of time, society, as we know it, has relentlessly tried to keep women in an invisible box, a mental chain. Historically a particular role has been assigned to women. One of housekeeper, wife, mother, cook, and cleaner, which she must diligently do in order to become a woman of virtue.

From Biblical history, we often see the lives and destinies of women in the kitchen and bedroom. Men are seen as world conquers. The most disturbing part about this is many women believe this lie, embracing it as their destiny.

For many of us, the narrative of our mothers' lives sounds like they were acting on an invisible script. Women find themselves groomed for domestication at an early age. As a young man, I witnessed girls told to do the dishes while their brothers played away as it was the proper thing to do.

As a result of early role assignments in childhood, especially firstborn girls, took the role of not just big sister but also a mini mother. These early role assignments were in preparation and grooming for a destiny society had written for women as homemakers. The girl child had no voice. Her aspirations and dreams were stolen until she stopped dreaming.

Then, when considered herself old enough, society once again stole her life, placing her in a marriage, whether she wanted it or not. Locked up in this little world, she's expected to be a domestic servant to her husband, with no voice.

Since the man has been appointed head of the home and the woman as his helpmeet, the only help society wants her to render is inside the house. Here she remains silent, complacent, and satisfied with everything she gets from her husband.

> **"It is not good for a man to be alone; I will make him a help meet for him."**
>
> **Genesis 2:18.**

The injustice women face today may be rooted in the term help meet. Yet, society has held on to this term with a tight fist, even from the ancient historical times recorded in the Bible.

Help meet in a lot of ways translated to, home help. This was regarded as a woman's ultimate purpose. We have been taught a man completes our lives and suffering breeds virtuousness. Yet women who were praised in the Bible based on biblical historical records, show they were those who were brave enough to go against the social norms of what a virtuous woman looks like. She was outside of the norm but often full of faith backed by God.

When she is not in the home being a wife, she becomes an object of lustful desires. Men have placed a price tag on her like a piece of meat. While used to satisfy the lust of the flesh, men tag her with different titles unworthy of her value such as gold digger, loose, and other derogatory labels and comments.

For some women using their bodies to entice a man for money is all she knows when it comes to survival in the world. So it is today that woman has been taught how to live. If the woman was not lucky enough to be married and utterly dependent on her husband, she had few options.

Her body has already been seen as a symbol of sex, just as chicken is seen as a delicious and appealing meal to many. We do not support defiling your body, but these women live the life they know. Unfortunately, they lack care and self-love.

Her consent to having her body traded for sex comes from a history of sexual abuse she dared not speak about. Knowledge to set her free that she was denied. As a result, her body became her tool for survival. She might take on menial jobs, but with the income that follows, it's only a matter of time before she gives in to the pressure.

Even when she tried to speak up, society made her believe she should see the advancement of the wolves seeking to devour her body as a compliment. For the woman, she had two options: be a wife or a sex tool. The bottom line is she would end up at the mercy of men. Most of whom are selfish.

These selfish laws against women have been passed down for many generations. The result, is an invisible form of bondage in women's minds, an invisible type of slavery. The woman was taught to look down when speaking, both in her mind and with her eyes. Sadly, some women believed this. They could no longer dream. They had a suffrage destiny written for them even before they were born.

But as time passed, more women rose above these limitations. More women began speaking up, daring to reach their full potential. The need for women to be more is the cry in their souls to fulfill their true purpose on earth.

However, there are still doubts in the minds of women. This mind cage is still prevalent to this day. While many women may feel the stir in their spirits to be more, they do not know how to move forward.

The widely felt discrimination by men leaves them confused and undecided on what to do with themselves. But the modern woman keeps pushing and fighting to change the longspoken selfish narrative.

First, let us look at the true meaning of help meet. The definition has been lost in a selfish translation. The word meet means equal, while help is called 'Ezar' in Hebrew. 'Ezar' is not tied to one word. It's better translated as one who is strong, rescues, and saves.

When God created woman, He made her a rescuer, savior, and strength to man. No wonder he used the man's rib to create a woman. The woman's creation process was unlike the man's. She was made from the rib of man, who was created in God's image.

The need for a woman's creation was to fill a void man and every other creature on earth could not fill. The woman was created to perfection from a perfectly finished material because part of her role was to be a strong vessel capable of complimenting, securing, and strengthening the man. She was made to perfect the good things of life, bringing meaning and light into man's life.

The woman was created after God rested and was built to perfection using a perfect finished product in God's image. The intended purpose was to be an equal partner for the man equipped with strength.

Therefore, while women and men may differ, we have all been equipped with special duties. Yet these duties do not put the woman beneath the man. Instead, they were made to complement one another.

In the past, few women were courageous enough to live up to God's standard of virtuousness. Those women not only had their footprints printed on the sands of time, but they had God's backing.

In the story of Esther, we discover a true definition of a virtuous woman. A humble maiden, whom God lifted above others, finding favor in the sight of the King.

She was also described as courageous. Hearing of a plan to kill her people, the Jews, When the King of Persia was about to be tricked into killing the Jews, she admonished her people to a time of fast. Following the fast, she met the King. The King listened as she laid her request before him, and the Jews were saved. God went ahead of her even before the King's meeting.

> **"Go, gather together all the Jews who are in Susa, and fast for me. Do not eat or drink for three days, night or day. My maids and I will fast as you do. I will go to the King when this is done, even though it is against the law. And if I perish, I perish."**
>
> **Esther 4:16**

One of the main criteria that made Esther stand out was her courage and her action. The oppression of the female gender required effort from the men. Therefore, to regain our birthright and become the virtuous woman of Proverbs 31, action is required. These actions make the necessary changes happen. The new era of women today is moving forward by taking action.

What Should A Woman Make Happen?

To make anything happen, the woman must first understand how uniquely she is made. She has to realize her body is holy and sacred.

> "Do you not know that your bodies are temples of the Holy Spirit, who is in you, whom you have received from God? You are not your own; you were bought at a price. Therefore, honor God with your bodies."
>
> **1Corinthians 6:19-20**

This passage speaks against sexual immorality and the debasement of the body. For a long time, men have made women believe their body was made for them. Sexual prowess gives women power and an advantage in society. But this is false, and the reverse is actually the case.

When a woman realizes how precious her body is, she commands respect from men and honors the Lord. A woman who chooses to honor her body creates more value for herself helping her prepare for the immense role God has prepared for her. It is our responsibility to carry ourselves as a queen, not reduce ourselves to the standards of others.

For centuries, a man has paraded himself as a provider for the woman. A virtuous woman must detest idleness to make change happen.

> **"She is a hard worker, strong and dynamic. She knows the value of everything she makes and works late into the night. She spins her thread and weaves her cloth."**
>
> **Proverbs 31:17-19.**

While working hard, we must also recognize the value of knowledge. Hosea 4:6, says, "My people are destroyed for lack of knowledge." Therefore, a woman who builds her intellectual capacity can move forward in society.

A woman who knows her worth and rights in Christ and society can never be intimidated. Even when others try to make her feel small, and talk down to her, she still raises her head up high. She is confident and persistent. This means women must surround themselves with edifying books and sources of knowledge.

She must recognize she is being watched and serve as an example for the women around her. The way she carries herself will become a motivation for others, leading to a path of redemption for many women.

Several women want to change the narrative. A woman who takes positive actions, becomes the savior for many other women, and our future daughters, from the bondage society places on them.

The Bible clearly describes the virtuous woman as a dynamic woman. Our talent and intelligence were not made for the kitchen and family alone. She serves value to herself and her community. She's an independent woman. To make this happen, we have to make deliberate decisions, train our brains, and teach our girl children, to aim for the stars instead of the kitchen.

Chapter - 2
CHART YOUR COURSE
Prioritize Work & Family
ACHIEVE MOVEMENT INC.
www.achieve-movementinc.ca

CHART YOUR COURSE:

Prioritize Work And Family

Bette Milder once said, "My idea of a superwoman is someone who scrubs her own floors."

The woman who scrubs her ownfloors is not necessarily the woman who drowns in domestic chores. A woman who cleans her own floors is a woman who gets things done. She could be described as a Proverbs 31:13 woman. "She seeketh wool, and flax, and worketh willingly with her hands."

Bette Milder's quote compliments the saying a woman's work is never done.' It is common knowledge young girls themselves are groomed quite early. Part of their childhood might be altered just to fit society's erroneous definition of a woman.

From a young age, the average young woman sees her brothers playing while she practices her domestic and self-grooming skills. Even as a child, her work starts and never seems to end. Her clothes are prettier than her brothers, and she spent more time on her hair. If she is the firstborn, she might even become the assistant mother.

As she grows older, her grooming becomes a little more intense. With the confusing stage of puberty, she then deals with raging hormones changing her body rapidly. At this stage, the focus on her, over her brothers, becomes even more intense.

She's now taught how to manage her menstrual flow and personal hygiene. Good personal hygiene is a good thing, but she's taught these things for the attention of men. With the onset of puberty, her curves and breasts become more protruded, and she becomes more aware of her sexuality.

Since she has been taught all her life to live for her purpose of being a wife, she begins to slowly and deliberately get the boys' attention. After years of practice, she can quickly spend more time on her hair and wearing outfits appearing appealing to the opposite sex.

As time passes, without properly realizing her identity, she charts the wrong life's course. She places priority on men and their approval. She wants to be seen and applauded, allowing

herself to be mentally imprisoned. The woman quickly centers her life goals on men and being the woman who fits the narrative, a people pleaser. This relatively shallow mentality and life goal come with dire consequences. Her whole life starts revolving around men. Living to be pleasing and attractive to them, little attention is placed on her brain and morals.

It gets worse because young women start seeing each other as competitors, trying to dress to outshine each other. It slowly feels like a contest. Suddenly they all work hard seeking the best scores from judges and positive reviews from the audience. This might be the root of jealousy and rivalry among women. For this reason, women start a meaningless battle against each other rather than creating a shield of love and unity.

The path the woman decides to take will speak into her life sooner or later. Then, as she becomes an adult with the introduction of makeup and more responsibilities, it becomes hard to keep up with the flashy lifestyle. The need to be a diva is more prevalent than ever. At this point, the charting of her course becomes the most critical decision she will ever make.

If she refuses to break from the shackles of mental slavery, she will lean upon the advances of men. It is important to note the average man enjoys the chase. He sees it as a game and the woman as prey. His satisfaction is getting the woman where he wants her on his bed. He is willing to give her what she wants in exchange for this desire.

Woman, Free Yourself from Captivity!

> "There is a way which seems right unto a man, but the end thereof is the ways of death."
>
> Proverbs 14:12

Often women find themselves living up to a certain standard, a standard usually above her means. Of course she will temporarily get the fast cars, the diva lifestyle, and attention from men she desperately craves. However, this is detrimental to her destiny.

> "Favor is deceitful, and beauty is vain: but a woman that feareth the LORD shall be praised."
>
> Proverbs 31:30.

It may sound cliché, but for some women, your life choices in finding a mate, reflects on you being treated only as baby mamas. This is not God's plan for the woman He created in excellence.

The reality of the woman's life starts dawning on her after she becomes a baby mother. Some women indeed prefer this lifestyle, thinking work is complex preventing them from being the kind of women men want to take home. The reverse is actually the case.

When a woman chooses this dangerous course, it's only a matter of time before her baby daddies abandons her. He eventually leaves her for another female, and she is left to fend for herself and her baby.

At this point, reality sets in. Now the idea of becoming a diva is left behind. Now the sole responsibility of parenting her child or children, becomes important.

The woman now finds herself juggling two or more jobs. At this point in her life, beauty becomes vain. She sees life more clearly. She may be able to chart a new course in the right direction, taking control of the wheel of her life. But it will take time. At this point, she's a wounded woman searching for clarification in life. She's tired and her short life has suddenly started to crawl.

> **"Be not deceived; God is not mocked: for whatsoever a man soweth, that shall he also reap."**
>
> **Galatians 6:7**

God intended a better life for the woman. Indeed, a woman's work is never done, but she can choose her work. The end result is hers to bear and hers alone. Woman, no man is coming to save you. You have been equipped with excellence and strength.

Women, it is time to break this prison mindset. The example of Esther from the Bible shows firsthand the reward of charting your course in the right direction. As a woman with an excellent spirit, prioritize your family and work. The virtuous woman can be seen   thriving in her business and family.

> **"She seeketh wool, and flax, and worketh willingly with her hands."**
>
> **Proverbs 31:13.**

The virtuous woman is not a damsel in distress. Her worth is timeless. She is not a modern woman, but is an honorable woman. She's an example of the grand design made by God. As a woman you must be bold enough to chart your course in the right direction. Contrary to what some people believe, a woman who prioritizes her work can also build a family.

Prioritizing work as well as your family provides security. "She is not afraid of the snow for her household: all her household is clothed with scarlet."

The chart a woman chooses influences how she handles the multiple jobs of wife, mother, cheerleader, soccer mom, nurse, adviser, and role model. A woman who takes up work along with her family, creates value for herself. She does not need to compete with her spouse. Instead, she finds herself as an asset to him.

> **"Her husband is known in the gates, when he sitteth among the elders of the land."**
>
> **Proverbs 31:23.**

God created woman as a companion for man. However, you are also equipped to fend for yourself, irrespective of your marital status. You cannot help someone else if you are not strong enough.

Charting the course of work equips you with a different kind of wisdom in building a home. Contrary to popular belief, you can effectively run your home as a working mother. Women may feel a stab of guilt for choosing themselves, but don't cave into those feelings. A woman as strong as you, changing the narrative, can choose to get help.

You are not a domestic slave, and our queens from the Bible we look up to show us it is okay to seek help. Our model woman in Proverbs 31:15 reveals this to us, **"... giveth meat to her household, and a portion to her maidens."**

She is a woman of excellence who works diligently with her hands. Her managerial work skills help her run her home effectively and efficiently. She understands the need for divided labor, even in the family. If her spouse is not in the picture, for whatever reason, she can easily navigate life with dignity. She is an independent woman.

A woman clothes herself in dignity when she prioritizes her work and family. When she honors the Lord in the midst of this, she becomes an unstoppable force. She is an example of God's original intent when created the woman.

Dear woman, strive for excellence. There may be truth to the saying, a woman's work may never end. But, working alongside her family, she is well on her way to a life of bliss and a dignified personality worthy of praise and emulation.

> **"Her children rise up and call her blessed; her husband also praises her. So many daughters have done virtuously, but thou excellent them all."**
>
> **Proverbs 31:28-29.**

Chapter - 3
HURDLES

The Many Roles You Play

HURDLES:
The Many Roles You Play

God created the woman with a unique type of strength and resilience. But society has given women many roles far from their ordained ones. These roles question her sanity, strength, stability, and purpose on earth. She has been given the position of mother, housewife, cook, cleaner, gardener, homemaker, nurse, psychologist, independent woman, meek, humble, patient, prayer warrior, grandmother, and many more.

First, her traditional role has been someone's property. The social error in this thinking says she must be of a calm and quiet spirit, a woman easily tossed around. At that point, when she is given the privilege of someone's wife, she must make magic happen.

The woman is expected to be patient with her irresponsible husband or boyfriend, or pray for him to change. It seems he's not accountable for his actions. Instead, the woman is blamed for his womanizing spirit because a good woman is expected to tame her husband.

She's expected to be a mother. Whether she wants this role or not or is prepared for it, it is not her choice. The destiny of motherhood has been drafted for her. When she has children, she becomes the sole caretaker, even when she is not a single mother.

She's expected to be the one the children look up to for support and guidance. But the woman was made to help the man, not be the man. She is expected to rise early, cook for the family, prepare the children for school, and do their homework.

If her children's father cannot pay the bills, she's expected to take up the responsibility. Unfortunately, little emphasis is placed on the man who cannot fulfill his duty as the man. Instead, it's expected the woman will pick up the slack.

She is expected to get the children looking properly for outings, and her job is to ensure they are wellmannered. At the same time, she's expected to pamper the man in her life, be it her husband, boyfriend, or her sons do not have a father figure in their lives.

Her capacity to be all these becomes the criteria for being labeled a good wife, mother, and woman. If she's a single mother, she's quickly blamed for being one, while the man is pardoned, usually starting a new life with another woman. But her ability to do the roles assigned to her without complaining is why society will forgive her pain. Oh, woman! Thou art loosed!

As time passes, more women are beginning to lose touch with this line of thinking. As a result, they started changing the roles written for them. They most likely saw their mothers and grandmothers before them, which helped shape their decision on the position they wanted to play.

She quickly realizes her birthright in society, at home, and with God, and begins to change the narrative. She became bold enough to pursue her desired career and nurture her talents.

Many women have chosen their core role as independence. However, with the harsh economic system, it is challenging to stay dependent on anyone. More women have taken a different superwoman approach to being financially independent and work on their intellect.

She has decided to take up the task of improving herself and creating a solid foundation for herself. Her dream isn't just to be a wife, but a woman of value impacting her world. Therefore, she has challenged herself to be educated and contribute to the economy.

Establishing a name for herself and her brand becomes her goal. She wants to be a financial woman with a character of her choosing. She's prepared to make the necessary sacrifices as a foundation for her future if she decides to have children.

When she has children, she can cater to the children's economic well-being without putting them in danger. She is the actual definition of a superwoman.

The real image of a woman commissioned by God!

She hears the saying society has written which says behind every successful man is a woman. But she changes the narrative to one of, besides every successful man is a woman. She refuses to take her brilliance and shove it behind a man, nurturing his dreams while hers go to waste.

In this way, the woman's strength is displayed. A strong woman standing by her husband, not behind him. The notion that a woman should be behind the man will pose a massive hurdle in the path toward success.

However, since it is her right to choose her path, some women are not brave enough to take on a better role. To date, some men still see women as sex symbols and will do anything to win them. It gives them pride like a hunter takes pride in catching his game.

These women feel that taking the traditional role is much easier. They are married to a man who becomes God over their lives, or they use their body in exchange for money.

To date, the sex business is a thriving one and more women continue to venture into this. Unfortunately, they derive joy in the fast cars and the diva lifestyle without a sustainable income to back it up.

For some women, using their bodies is much easier, and they don't see the need to be of value. Instead, they believe men craving after their bodies like an ant for sugar is valuable.

They see the debasement on their body as love. They feel prioritizing work and family is too much work and stress. They think it will take the fun away. To them, working is too much hassle. They believe men are built to be successful, and women are created to be behind them.

But unbeknownst to them, this life path only leads to more demanding rules. Whatever a man sows he will reap. The fruit of their labor always follows a pattern.

Since that set of women sees working on their career as work, they tend to lavish their money on expensive lifestyles. Soon, they become baby mamas for deadbeat fathers.

But it doesn't end there. After a while, the women continue to birth more babies because they have to continue to sleep around to earn money for themselves and their kids. After a while, they end up with many children from multiple fathers.

Alas! Beauty is vain. Her beauty begins to fade, and reality dawns on her.

Now, she takes the role of a struggling father and mother. She must provide them with shelter, food, clothing, security, healthcare, emotional support, and education.

She ends up handling multiple jobs to keep up with the bills. As a result, her life becomes complex and discolored Sooner or later, her kids take to the street fending for themselves.

Whatever role a woman chooses to play will determine the life she will live for the rest of her life.

Excluding women from the Bible, modern Queens like Sarah Jakes Roberts and Joyce Meyer chose the path leading to a successful future. They took action and did what must be done. Today, their results are here for the whole world to see.

Dear woman, when you turn grey and leave the earth, what legacy do you hope to leave for future generations? The reality of your answer is determined by the role you choose to play.

Chapter - 4
INTENSITY

You Make It Happen

INTENSITY:
You Make It Happen!

As a woman, the intensity of your life is determined by the role you choose to play. The life of a woman can either be struggling or a life eating from hand to mouth. In this life path, her tomorrow is not guaranteed, and she works multiple jobs to make ends meet. She has no purpose but to put food on her table for herself and her kids. She has little or no creativity left in her. A life where she is invisible in her workplace and does the bidding of everyone to survive.

Or her life can be one where she makes things happen. A life is driven by purpose and passion. A life where her children and other women look up to her as a role model. Someone worthy of emulation. A life where she calls the shots. She speaks, and people listen. She enters a room, and the place falls silent. She is the boss. She lives life as a legend, leaving a lasting legacy for others.

This type of woman must rise above her circumstances. She must be able to heal, letting go of any baggage weighing her down. To make this happen as a woman, you must be willing to live your life to your full potential, even while pursuing your career dreams and caring for your family.

The most fantastic thing about this is any woman, irrespective of cultural background or life history, can intensify her life's goals and make things happen for her.

Hayley is one such lady who makes things happen. She was born differently able and was offered the best in life to make her as comfortable as they could. Her life story has not been the fairy tale type, but she is strong. She's an excellent example of a woman who decided to make things happen in her life.

She lost her mother at a point in her life, and her father was somewhat distant as he lived in another country. This challenge is enough to keep anyone down. But, as I said earlier, anyone can choose to make something happen, despite the situation.

In addition to a rough life and her

disabilities, she became a single mother. These circumstances around her are less than the reasons some women choose to throw in the towel and settle for a life of struggles.

But she determined to make something happen against all odds. She removed the hurdles from her life by accepting the loss of her mother. Losing a loved one affects a person deeply. Losing a loved one hurts and leaves us finding them in people who take advantage of our vulnerability. She accepts it and also forgives her father for his inability to be present.

Letting go of all that weight, she takes on self-love. Every woman needs selflove to succeed. It is impossible to enter a room and get things done without the confidence coming with self-love. She could love herself by understanding Jesus first loved her, even before she was born. She was made in the image and likeness of God. As a result, irrespective of her physical looks, she was made to perfection just like that!

What a woman! Finding her driving force and confidence in God, she makes a decision to step into her destiny. This pushes her to keep entering rooms many are intimidated to enter. She prioritizes her work and her family. They are both precious in her sight. She has been a source of inspiration for me to get things done. If she can, so can I.

As a woman who has decided to make it happen, you will need to put in the effort at work as much as you do to your family. To make an impact at your job, you have to work full-time. You must double the effort unless you want to be like everyone else, stagnant with nothing to show. There are no shortcuts. Moving forward making a lasting impact includes working during the day and reading at night.

Being a mother does not make it

easier. You must balance your relationship with your kid(s) while bringing excellence to work. Alas, working tirelessly at the job is not enough. Otherwise, you find yourself working more and remaining stagnant.

While you put in the hours, you have to get a higher degree to get your desired promotion resulting in higher pay. Lacking efficiency and effectiveness is not an option with the higher degree you are reaching for. The only option you have is to opt for a night class.

The sacrifice you pay to make it happen might look steep, but the reward is highly satisfying. Failure to make it happen leaves you working hard with little results until you retire. The consequences are dire.

While you take action on your dreams, you must also support your family and children. A mother who fails to be a mother is not truly successful, despite her success in her corporate life. The virtuous woman we try to emulate in Proverbs 31 does excellently with her job and her family.

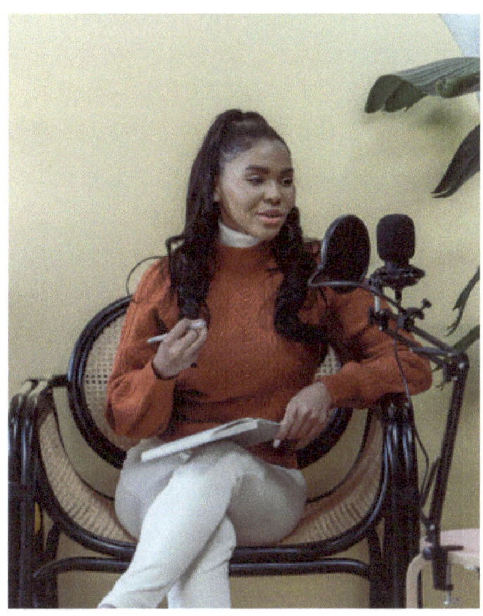

> **"She looketh well to the ways of her household, and eateth not the bread of idleness."**
>
> **Proverbs 31:27.**

In modern times, you ensure homework is done, show up for school meetings and other school activities. You do not show up for your children to fulfill all righteousness. You show because you love your children and love supporting them.

Your boss should not be the only person with your attention and listening ears. The bond between you and your children must be unbreakable. Children are watching and listening. For your children to be the adult's society desperately needs,

you must be their best friends. This means making sure you make time to talk with them.

Teach them about the Word of God and their sexuality. Your success as a mother is significant. Just as you try to break the barrier of mental slavery with your actions today, you prevent it in the future with your impact on your kids now. They see you as a superwoman and learn they can be all that and sustain a family.

As you continue to be a super mom and employee, your night school exams eventually start knocking. Now the extra effort is required in your studies, preparing adequately for exams. Your sleep and daytime will be sacrificed.

But it does not end there. Your exams may fall in the middle of a deadline for a job. Trust that the devil will play tricks and one child, particularly the youngest, may fall sick. This means, the woman must shuffle and balance her job, exam, and home.

It can be challenging for any woman, and it might seem like a good time to give up and face your family. But this is the moment to intensify your efforts. Remember it is the darkest before dawn.

Always remember, your quest to live life in Christ is not just about money. It's about the satisfaction of standing tall amid adversity. Every woman who decides to make it happen sets a noble example for other women globally.

Nothing motivates a woman to push more than the success of another woman. This means, there is no time to complain. Instead, when it feels overwhelming, you take on the challenge and take courage from **Philippians 4:13, "I can do all things through Christ, which strengthens me."**

A strong woman is not afraid to ask for help. Asking for help for your child does not make you a weak mother but a good mother. If physical support is unavailable, there's always a way out when you look closely enough. Where there's a will, there's a way.

In the end, resilient, you will pass your exams after the obstacles, no matter how hard it might be. It might seem impossible when the challenge comes, but you can make everything happen.

Meanwhile, your hard work is being felt at your place of work. The promotion you desire may be delayed as part of the challenges in the organization, but your efforts will be undeniably felt.

It can get scary knowing there are people in the workplace ready to pull you down to caress your ego. But hard work is always felt and seen by others.

After you send your new certificate after passing your exams, you will be well-qualified for the position.

Even if your boss is against you, you can do all things through Christ who strengthens you. Even if there's no opening for a promotion, everybody loves value. Everyone needs value. The bosses will see your effort and will not mind creating a space for you to fill.

You will get the recognition and promotion you deserve. Your effort and intensity will make you find fulfillment at work and in your family. No amount of complaints, tears, or pity can make it happen. Only your intensity and effort make the things in your life happen.

In the first four chapters of this book, I've tried to illustrate using the examples given in the bible of a virtuous woman to present a guide for my daughters and women to follow. As a man, I cannot speak to all the challenges that women go through in their lives. I've invited Ms. Domonique Alicia Bradford to co-author the remaining chapters with me.

Chapter - 5
EFFORTS

No Rest In Your Nest

EFFORTS:
No Rest In Your Nest!

When I think about a woman's duty, I compare it to a bird's nest. The bird first builds her nest in a place she considers safe for herself and her new chicks and her family. She spends the entire day gathering materials for building her nest, while hunting for food for herself. She does all this while also staying safe.

After successfully building her nest, it becomes her haven, and she lays her eggs. Yet, even with her eggs laid, she manages to keep them warm and provide food for herself too.

When the eggs hatch, the mummy bird does not relax to enjoy the fruit of her labor yet. She still looks for food for her newborn and herself. Even while she's out fending for her family, her interests are still at home. She checks up on her chicks often and gives them food.

After the hustle and bustle, she returns to the nest to be with her chicks. As they grow older, she teaches them to fly. If necessary, catches them when they fall, while fending for herself at the same time. She continues this routine until her chicks leave the nest to find their way.

I often think about her life and survival skills if she decided to be with her chicks without leaving the nest after her baby's hatch. The fact she hunts for herself and her babies makes her a skilled hunter. Her survival skills and instincts become heightened.

The life of the mother bird can be likened to a woman. To reach and maintain her success, she continues working.

When a woman reaches higher heights of success, she continues to understand her work is never done. Therefore, after making things happen, she must be ready to sustain what she has achieved to achieve even more.

Lack of sustenance will eventually make you redundant and at risk of going back to where you started. You need continual growth in your workplace and your relationship with your family. They balance each other. None is more vital than the other.

Of course, taking a break now and then from official duties is welcome, as it gives you time to rest and refresh. But this much-desired break is only short-lived. Ironically, any break from work to spend with family creates a standard that must be upheld. Such responsibilities for women!

Many believe life is like the fairy tales we read as children. The promotion comes and it's smooth sailing for the rest of your life. The late Dr. Myles Munroe refers to life as being in a boxing ring. Life throws you a few punches, the bell rings giving you time to rest, and then you go again.

In the midst of the excitement, you decide to take the family on a vacation celebrating and spending quality time with them. After all, in their way, they are your support system. They deserve to enjoy the wins with you. The trip gives you time to set new goals and bond with your children. The time spent is of high quality. They were many family games, they took pictures, and you got to rest. At that point, it felt like work no longer exists. The only thing that matters is living in the moment enjoying family and fun.

However, as life would have it for the woman, there is little rest in her nest.

She returns from her much-needed break, which was a reward for her hard work. Since being promoted from project associate to the project manager.

Getting back, feeling energized and refreshed, what was supposed to be her happy time, she's greeted with unpleasant news at work. Two of her project leads were let go following a physical altercation during her absence. At this point, the guilt of taking time off weighs heavy. She wonders how and why it happened. The staff no longer there, occupied significant positions on her team and were crucial in making the right things happen.

With no time to ask questions, it is time to get back to work. The company has not started the replacement process yet, so you now lead by yourself as the newly appointed manager. Your time management and leadership skills are on full display. While being the cheerleader leader at the extra curriculum activities for your kids and the after-school teacher for their assignments, all eyes are on you to deliver your assigned duty efficiently and effectively.

Assigning the duties of the former staff to others was not an option. For productivity's sake, you take over the job. As a result, the weight of your official duties becomes five times more intense. With all this, you still need to care for your young children. Maintaining the bond you already shared with the children was paramount. But it's also the most hectic time in your life.

There was no rest, and sleep starts feeling like a luxury vacation. Then just when you thought it couldn't get any more demanding, it does.

This almost chaotic life of zero rest and endless responsibilities helps shape you into the woman you aspire to be. It enables you to realize the

challenges a woman must overcome, preparing her for a higher feat. Therefore, God will not give you specific promotions until you are ready.

You must set realistic goals, both short and long-term. You have always been a time-conscious individual, but these are some intense realities the career woman encounters on her way to the top. In all this, you must be aware of your anger and manage it well. When things don't go your way, you must be rational because the outcome depends on your reaction.

You may not realize it, but the many demands life places on you propel you to do everything with excellence. As a result, you are well on your way to becoming clean refined gold and a queen worthy of her crown.

Taking care of elderly parents and young children is another acute exposure to teaching patience when placed in a management position. It brings out the thoughtful side of you to understand if you are battling all these real-life issues, the people under your command might be dealing with similar or even worse situations. This is good to incorporate into your people- patient skills in the workplace. Your managerial skills will also play a

significant role in getting things done at home in an orderly fashion. Indeed, my decision to prioritize work and family was building me to become the help meet I was created to be.

The scenarios might be different, but it is the same story and pattern for women. If you prioritize one aspect of your life and leave the other, it doesn't make the duty less demanding.

The rest you desire in the nest will continue to elude you. It is because God created us to be more, strong. Just like workouts, you must do it consistently to see desired results. The more weight you carry, the stronger you become.

Women who are yet to be tested might often wonder how others manage to cope with balancing their lives. We have been created with the strength and capacity to do these things. As often as we crave rest in our nest, our work and family give us a sense of satisfaction, fulfillment, and warmth we cannot fully explain.

We have been called with the ability to excel in both areas. Sooner than later, you begin to understand the purpose of your seemingly challenging situation. As I said, the case might differ for every woman, but it's the same story.

The Proverbs 31 woman shows us there is always work to do. She excelled in all. You too can take the responsibilities gracefully like the Queen you are. Our nests have been created to stay awake, at least until we have reached our full potential.

Proverbs 31:10-31 describes a strong virtuous woman capable in all aspects of life. She's a hard worker, managing her household, caring for her family, and even running her own business. She is also wise, kind, and respected by her husband and children. The passage is often seen as an example of the ideal woman, who balances her responsibilities and excels in everything she does.

The message in this passage tells us we are capable of great things, and we should embrace our responsibilities with grace and determination. We should strive to be like the woman described in Proverbs 31, who works tirelessly to provide for her family, while also making a positive impact in her community.

It's important to note the passage does not mean a woman has to do everything perfectly or that she can't ever rest. But it encourages us to be hardworking, diligent, and to strive for excellence in all aspects of our lives.

Being a queen is not just a title or a status, but a mindset. It's about taking charge of our lives and being the best version of ourselves. It means embracing our responsibilities with grace and determination while aiming for excellence in everything we do. It's about being confident in our abilities and not afraid to take on new challenges.

Being a queen also means being a leader, not only in our personal lives but also in our communities. It's about setting a positive example for others and being a role model for young women. It's about being a strong, capable, wise woman respected and admired by others.

Remembering that being a queen does not mean being perfect is also important. It's about aiming for excellence, while also being kind, compassionate, and understanding toward ourselves and others. We all have our own unique strengths and weaknesses and it's important to understand and accept these.

In short, being a queen is not just a status. It's a mindset and a way of life. It's about being a strong, capable, wise woman, aiming for excellence, and making a positive impact on those around you. It's about embracing our responsibilities and reaching our full potential as women.

Chapter - 6
VALUES
Established Environment

VALUES:
Established Environment

One of the vital lessons I've learned about hard work is it helps you find yourself and understand your cause. Since you have decided to place work and family side by side, you will always try to make time for both. As you do so, your creativity begins to emerge, and the excellence in your spirit blooms.

There is dignity in labor. One of the gains of working wholeheartedly to fulfilling your dreams is the solid foundation you lay for yourself for future heights. God also instructs us to work hard and be truthful to ourselves.

"Not with eyeservice, as men-pleasers; but as the servants of Christ, doing the will of God from the heart;

With good will doing service, as to the Lord, and not to men:

> **Knowing that whatsoever good thing any man doeth, the same shall he receive of the Lord, whether he be bond or free."**
>
> **Ephesians 6:6-8**

Historically, women who reached for success and established an environment suitable for them, helped them reach their full potential in a unique way. The thing about the woman is she was created with the ability to make and multiply life.

'Life' in this context is not limited to only childbearing but all areas of life. Since something needs to happen for life to be created, so does life in her career. The sleepless nights, continuing education, and extra hours she put into her job will soon become her motivation for her, creating different value systems.

After the woman has gained her promotion to a certain height, she will begin to need more. The need for more is because of her instinct for creativity and her excellent spirit. When she gets her promotion and starts making things happen, she will crave a better working environment.

People will always undermine her worth even after she has proved herself worthy. At first, her goal is to prove herself, but after she does, her need to make more impact begins to boil and emerge.

As a woman aiming for success, people in higher positions will always tell you what you should do, even if it is against what you propose. Your ideas are only as good as what the bosses want, even if it goes against what you want or stand for. She is only as good as the task before her. At this point, she begins to feel small again.

She wants an environment where she can be seen and heard. Yes, she has made her mark where she is, but it is based on someone else's ideas. Her spirit now wants to be free. She wants to be in charge of her time and earn higher respect for what she does.

She was a young plant wanting to grow irrespective of the soil. It was not her time to spread her branches wide. Oh! How I love growth! As she grows, the space becomes too small, and she notices a roof preventing her from growing tall.

For the woman, it becomes more challenging to spend quality time with her children following her promotion. She finds herself always making up for missing vital memories of their lives. When she gets home, she is too tired, or the children are asleep to spend time with her.

As she continues on this rollercoaster of missed time with her family, she soon loses her balance and starts losing the bond she already developed with them. Children grow up quickly. It doesn't matter how much money you bring home. It's the memories they will hold on to.

Children see things around them. As young adults, they might be compelled to have a little resentment towards work because they feel it steals them away from their mother, especially the female children.

It starts with the little things like missing bedtime stories, to finding out they had their first period days after it started. The relationship with your children can be fickle. They cherish your time with them over the luxury makeup gifts.

Before you know it, they are out of the nest, and it will be almost impossible to get the bond back. These are usually the reasons to establish a better environment, taking charge of your life and time.

To create an ideal environment the woman may aspire to become her own boss working for herself giving her the opportunity to manage and control her time. Historically, women of value always start this way before standing on their own to make a difference in the world.

Dr. Elizabeth Blackwell fought beyond all odds, becoming the first woman to receive a medical degree from an American medical school. She made her way into an all-male institution and financed medical school.

Her experience prompted her to open a women and children infirmary and a medical school for women doctors and people living in poverty. First, she started to get her degree to prove herself worthy. Then went ahead to create opportunities for other women making her mark on the sands of time.

For the woman, her newly established environment helps her create a transferrable legacy. She gets to do her thing without anyone discouraging her. This is truly the way a woman makes an impact in her world.

But don't get things mixed up. Without the proper foundation, the woman would be unable to create this environment for herself. Irrespective of her aspirations, proving herself and putting all her efforts into her nest prepare her for this. No amount of dreams can make up for the experience.

With this new boss role, the stars are only her starting point. She gets to spend quality time with her kids and continues from where she left off. Her children experience firsthand the work and sacrifice their mother makes for them. This helps put a lot of things into perspective for her kids.

She still has a lot of work ahead of her to turn the newly established environment into her legacy and creativity. She's ready to make it a physical representation of her mental projection, a great starting point for her end goal.

Chapter - 7

EARN -
Respect Rightfully!

EARN-
Respect Rightfully!

Now, the woman finds herself in her element. She is proud of herself for what she has accomplished thus far and is ready to work to make her stand out. The work and sacrifices she placed for herself, and her goals have paid off. Starting her own company was, indeed, the easiest part. She already knew the ropes. With her experienced team, her company was set up to her standard, now it is time to take over the world.

Due to her status as a mother, she developed an incredible threshold for having patience with people. Coupled with her excellent work history, it was relatively easy for her to maintain a good relationship with clients over time.

Can you imagine all that women have gone through and endured. Working hard to achieve success to earn their rightful respect in society.

The following scenario speaks of one such woman with an incredible confidence level in her job. With her skillset, she has been invited to submit a bid on a large project.

In no time she drafts a bid proposal to present to her soon-to-be investor. But she was not alone in this. As expected, she had competition wanting the same investor.

After putting the necessary things into place, she schedules a meeting with her potential investor. She feels confident and assured this will be the start of a profitable journey for her and her company.

Oblivious to her, she's about to get the shock of her life. On getting there, she meets her competition, waiting to meet the same client to present his bid proposal. Unfortunately, he was her school teacher!

The same teacher who told her she would not amount to anything meaningful. He assured her she wouldn't be able to graduate and she could also drop out. Due to her multiple commitments in other areas of her life, she didn't have the best grades in school or maximum concentration.

Of course, it was only natural to draw such students closer and be a source of encouragement. But, alas! She was not very likable to him. Besides, to him, in the end, she was a woman made for roles that may make her certificate redundant. As a result, he considered her a failure without giving her a chance to try.

They recognized each other as soon as they met in the investor's office. She was engulfed in mixed emotions. She never thought she would see him again. But here she was, sitting opposite him.

She never felt more proud in her life. She had wins, but this one felt different. She felt like she didn't just make herself proud but won the respect she deserved.

He was covered in shame and embarrassment. She exchanged pleasantries with him. But, as much as she would love to boast, it was not worth it. After all, all through her hard work, when it felt overwhelming, one of her favorite quotes remained "I can do all things through Christ which strengthens me" (Phillipans 4:13).

One of the most remarkable things about a virtuous woman is her humility. She understands God is the source of her strength and her successes come from Him alone.

After the pleasantries, her former teacher apologized for his ill behavior towards her in the past. But she had already forgiven him before he apologized because she is kind and knows her worth.

They went on to talk about their journey so far and how they ended up where they were together. They later bid on their proposal individually.

Her years of hard work and resilience began speaking for her during her proposal. She and her team carefully

drafted something unique that could stand the test of time.

Although the board she presented to was an all-men board, her experience with situations like that made her stand tall. After the proposal bid by her and her competitors, even in a dominant male space, her value could not be ignored or denied. On the contrary, it was glaring that she was suitable for this job. She won the project and it was a huge stepping stone for her newly established company. She was even able to offer her former teacher a consulting position in her firm. She wanted his expertise as he also needed to be on her team for productivity.

From that day on her company began florishing. She had a steady stream of clients, and her business was growing at an impressive rate. She had finally achieved her dream of owning her own business, which she had done with hard work and determination.

But more importantly, she had earned the respect of her peers and clients in the industry. She worked tirelessly to build her business and did it with integrity and humility. She was a role model for other women and showed them they too could achieve their dreams if they were willing to work for it.

Her story is a testament to the fact that with hard work and determination, anyone can achieve their goals and earn the respect they deserve. She had faced many challenges along the way, but she never gave up. She remained focused and worked tirelessly to achieve her dream.

In the end, it was her perseverance and her ability to overcome obstacles that led to her success. Even now she

continues to inspire and empower other women in her industry, showing them they too can earn the respect rightfully.

EPILOGUE

There will always be people in your life who will undermine your abilities at every stage. They have been wired that way and choose to succumb to the slavery of the mind. But do not let that pull you down. You are a product of resilience. Your mother and your mother's mother are all products of you. You come from a royal lineage of strong women.

There is someone inside of you screaming to be unleashed. The person is screaming to be seen and heard. The voice calling is the voice of our mothers who never got the chance to be more. It is the voice of our sisters who told us to remain silent and smile at their abusers.

Nothing will ever change if we do not take action now. Some women from our past stood up and fought for their rights. Some fought for the right to get a degree.

While some fought to give the female child equal career opportunities in medicine, males have dominated this area for centuries. But when one woman fought for it, others joined the course, and change happened.

The courage of women from our past rubbed off on other courageous women fighting for the rights of other women, both living and dead. Some call them feminists, while others call them activists. But their fight opened the doors of civil rights we enjoy today.

Women from our past made it easier for us today to be more. It opened more opportunities to make things happen. Why not ditch any excuse you might have and work on yourself today?

You must remember we were made to be equal with man. While you might face the sting of sexism, it is only part of the hurdle to jump to the side of success. But it is not the end. It doesn't matter the difficulties surrounding you. Other women have faced such problems, and they made things happen.

Woman, your children are watching. Other females around you are watching. Take the bold step today to be more. This book, ACHIEVE-MA'AM, will help guide you through the hurdles you will face and other women whose lives you can learn from.

Starting today, surround yourself with the right people. Surround yourself with people who have passed through whatever fear you may have. Your brain is your tool, not your body. Your body is the temple of God and should only be shared with a man worthy of it.

In all your getting, the Word of God must be your companion as long as you live. It carries the original manual you need to pass through life. Proverbs 31 gives clear insight into the kind of woman we ought to be.

The earlier you take action to be the woman you dream of, the earlier you will arrive at your desired place. Remember you can do all things through Christ who strengthens you. I am rooting for you, and I am sure you will make the right things begin to happen, putting your excellent spirit to good use.

ABOUT THE AUTHOR

WARREN ANDREW PINDER

Prepare to be inspired by the captivating journey of Warren Andrew Pinder—a multifaceted visionary who has seamlessly woven the threads of leadership, literature, and life experience into a remarkable tapestry of accomplishments.

At the heart of Warren's narrative lies his profound dedication to unlocking the potential within every individual. As an accomplished writer and the creative mind behind the enlightening book,

"Achieve-Men," he has artfully delved into the intricate web of human dynamics. With a keen eye for detail and an insatiable thirst for knowledge, Warren has meticulously explored the intricate roles that men and women play in both society and the family. This exploration has been not just an academic endeavor, but a deeply personal one, fueled by his role as a loving husband and devoted father to six children and three grandchildren. These intimate connections have bestowed upon him invaluable insights, breathing life into his literary pursuits.

Beyond his prowess as an author, Warren's diverse portfolio of accomplishments takes center stage. An accomplished construction manager with decades of experience, he has seamlessly balanced his professional career with his commitments as the esteemed President of The Scout Association of the Bahamas and the influential Chairman of the National Junkanoo Committee. His leadership in these roles has left an indelible mark on his community, reflecting his dedication to preserving and celebrating cultural heritage.

A man of unwavering faith, Warren's Christian devotion serves as a compass guiding his beliefs and actions. His writings courageously tackle issues of cultural bias and self-discovery, extending a heartfelt invitation to individuals to rise above societal expectations and unearth their true selves.

Away from the world of words and responsibilities, Warren finds solace in the embrace of nature. An ardent lover of Junkanoo, he's drawn to the rhythms of life and the exuberance of celebrations. His affinity for the water is palpable— whether it's gracefully navigating the waves on a boat or immersing himself in the joyous embrace of a refreshing swim.

Eager to share his wealth of knowledge and insights, Warren welcomes you to join him on his online platforms. Discover his world of wisdom, inspiration, and thought- provoking ideas at **warrenandrewpinder.com** and **achieve-movementinc.ca.** Through his words and experiences, he beckons you to embark on a journey of self-discovery, empowerment, and unbridled achievement.

ABOUT THE AUTHOR

DOMONIQUE ALICIA BRADFORD

Prepare to be inspired by the remarkable journey of Domonique Alicia Bradford—an exceptional individual whose talents span the realms of both the written word and the world of numbers.

A true luminary, Domonique shines brightly as the gifted author behind "Repositioning the Mind for Prosperity." Her words have the power to reshape perspectives and inspire transformative growth. But her literary prowess doesn't stop there—she's also a driving force behind "Achieve-Mam," a collaborative endeavor that encapsulates her unyielding commitment to publishing and fostering empowerment.

From a young age, the world of accounting captured Domonique's curiosity, and over time, it became her true north. Her intimate familiarity with the financial industry, cultivated since childhood, sets her apart as a master in her field. With a natural acumen for numbers and an unwavering dedication to her craft, Domonique navigates the intricate landscape of finance with unparalleled expertise.

Yet, Domonique's impact reverberates far beyond spreadsheets and ledgers. As the visionary founder of the Warmina Foundation, she's committed to transforming lives. Through this noble organization, Domonique lends a helping hand to newcomers and minorities in Canada, guiding them along the path to discovering their true career potential. Her work isn't just a testament to her compassion—it's a living testament to her profound belief in the strength of unity and empowerment.

Domonique's journey to success has been nothing short of remarkable. As a single woman who has defied odds and shattered glass ceilings, she serves as a beacon of inspiration for others striving to carve their own paths. Her story is a living testament to the limitless potential within each of us to achieve greatness, regardless of the obstacles we face.

Beyond her professional pursuits, Domonique's zest for life shines through in her love for travel, connecting with new souls, and embracing fresh skills. Her insatiable curiosity is the driving force behind her relentless quest for growth and self-discovery.

Feeling compelled to join her on this incredible journey? The door is wide open. Visit the Warmina Foundation website at

warminafoundation.com

to discover how you can play a role in this noble mission. Domonique's story is an invitation—a call to action—to be part of a movement that uplifts, empowers, and reshapes the narrative for a brighter future.

Achieve Ma'am

AFFIRMATIONS

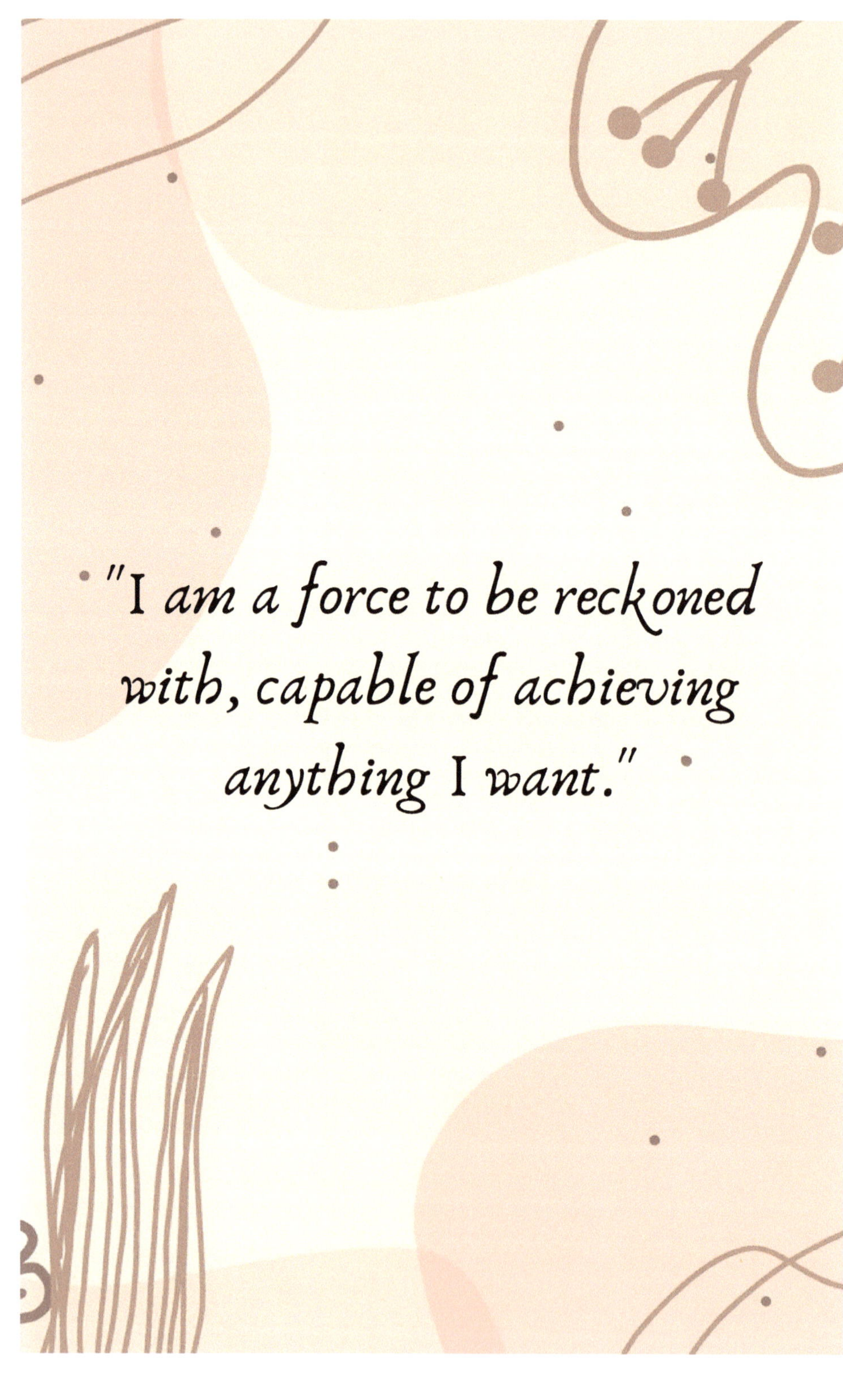
"I am a force to be reckoned with, capable of achieving anything I want."

AFFIRMATIONS

AFFIRMATIONS

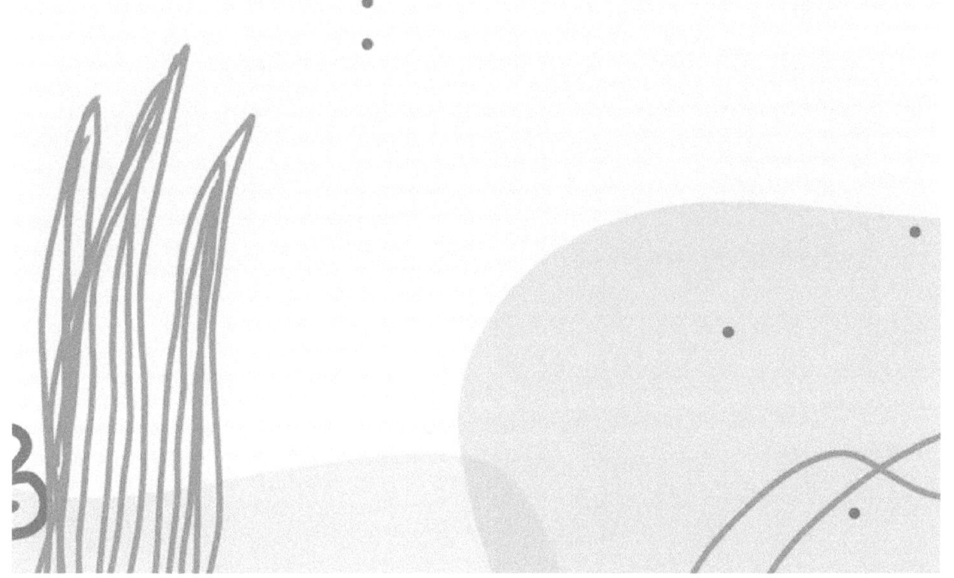

"I refuse to let anyone else's limitations or negativity hinder me from achieving my dreams."

AFFIRMATIONS

ACHIEVE MA'AM

AFFIRMATIONS

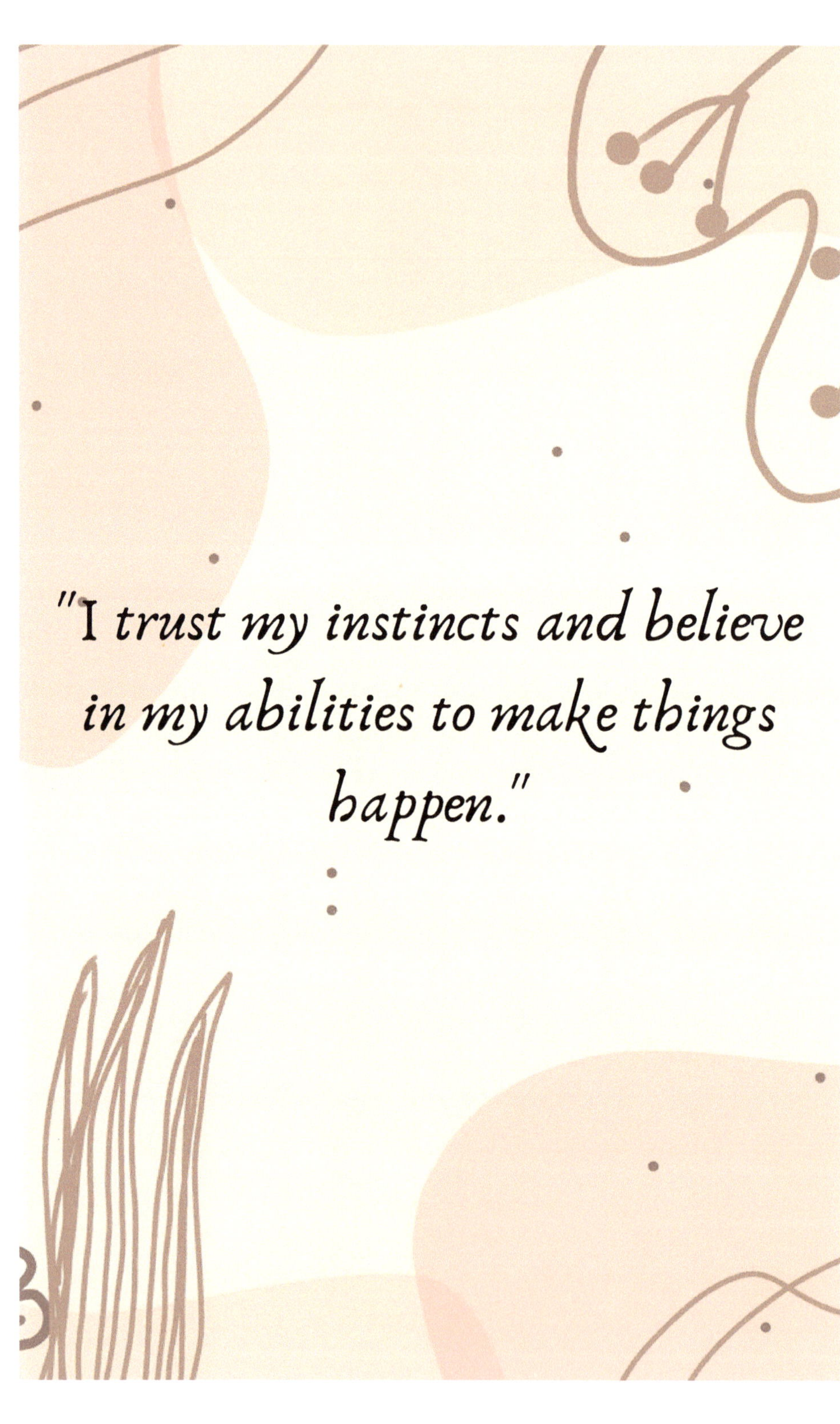

"I trust my instincts and believe in my abilities to make things happen."

AFFIRMATIONS

AFFIRMATIONS

"I am confident and fearless in pursuing my goals, and I will not let any obstacle stand in my way."

AFFIRMATIONS

AFFIRMATIONS

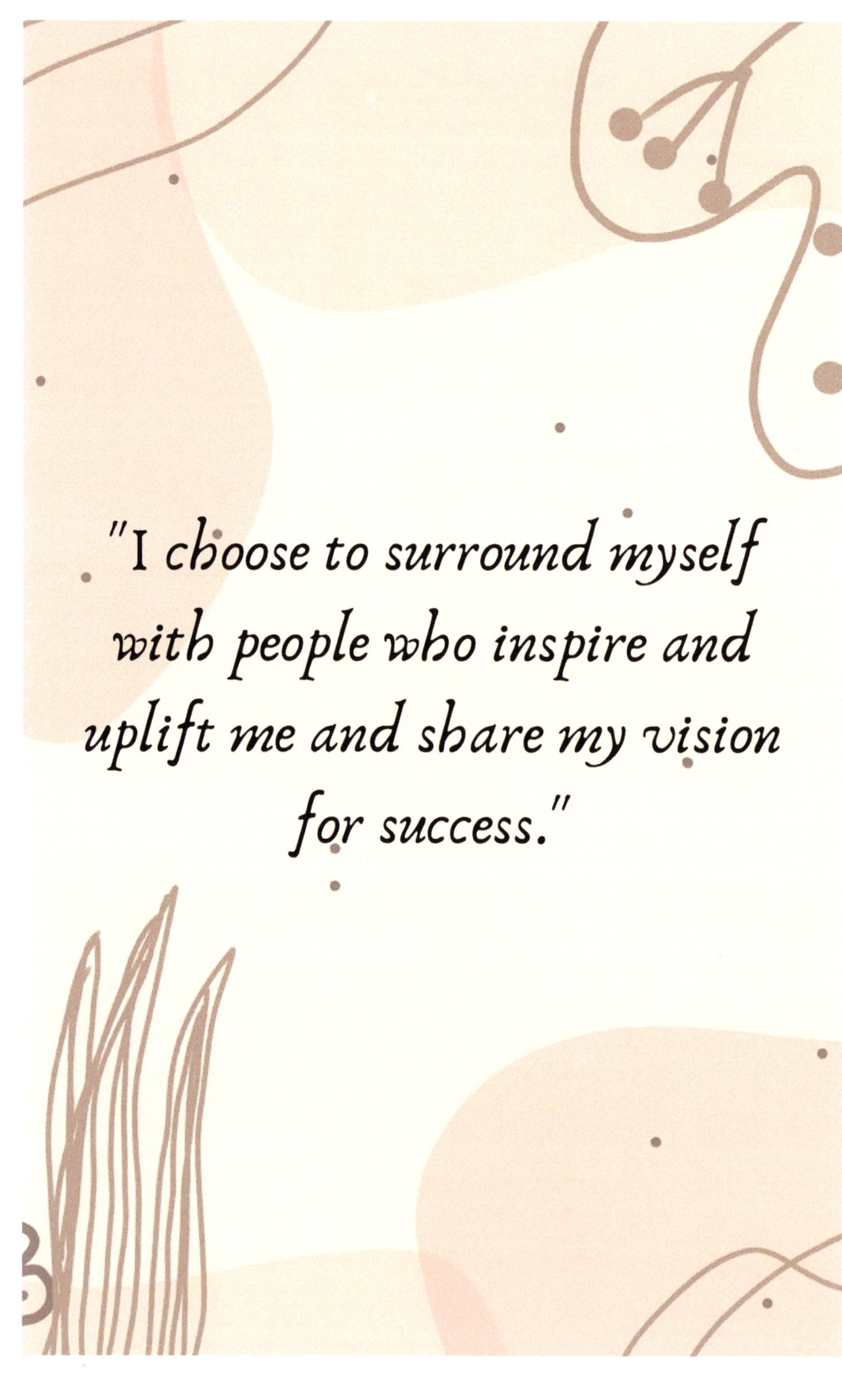

"I choose to surround myself with people who inspire and uplift me and share my vision for success."

AFFIRMATIONS

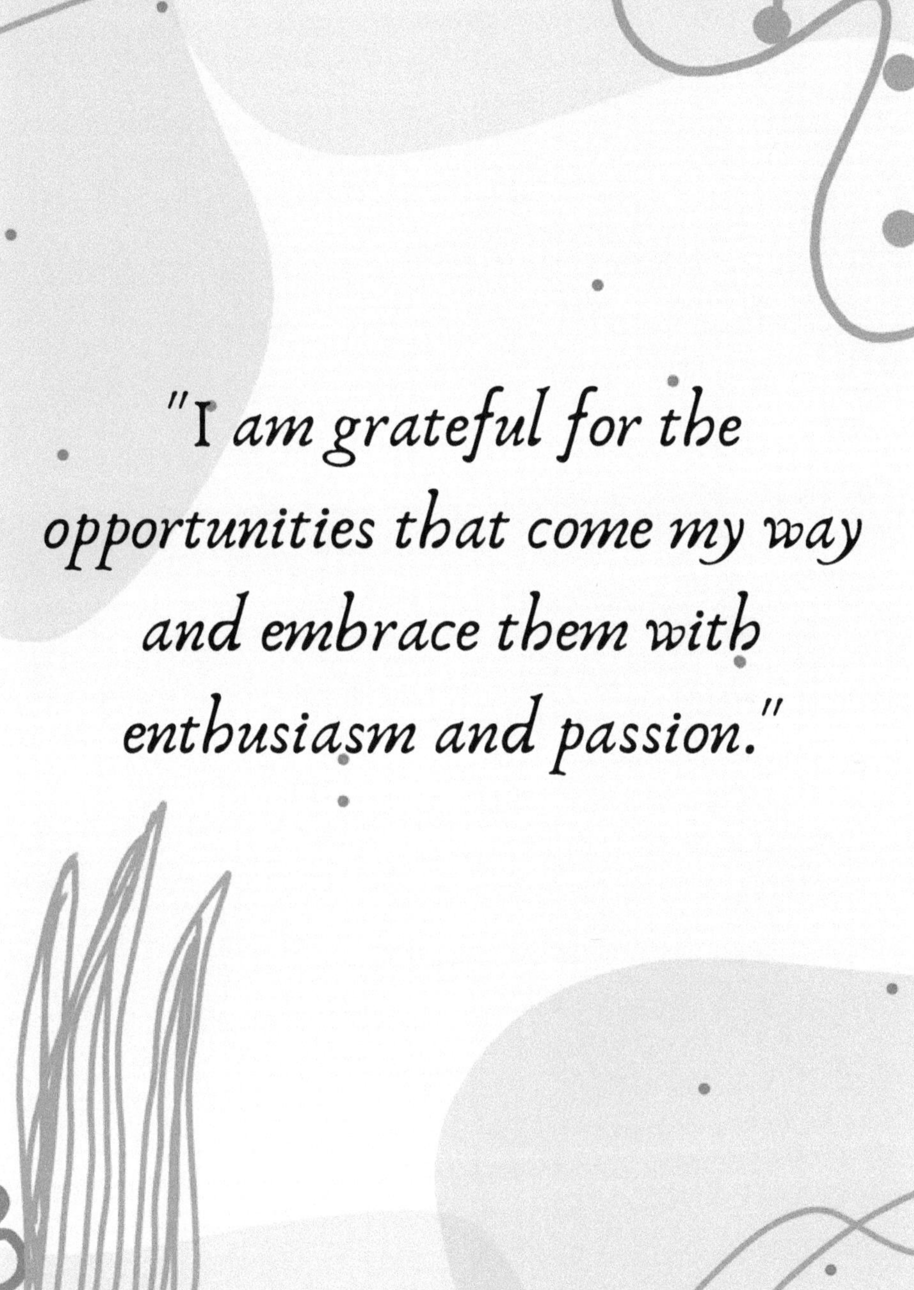
"I am grateful for the
opportunities that come my way
and embrace them with
enthusiasm and passion."

AFFIRMATIONS

ACHIEVE MA'AM

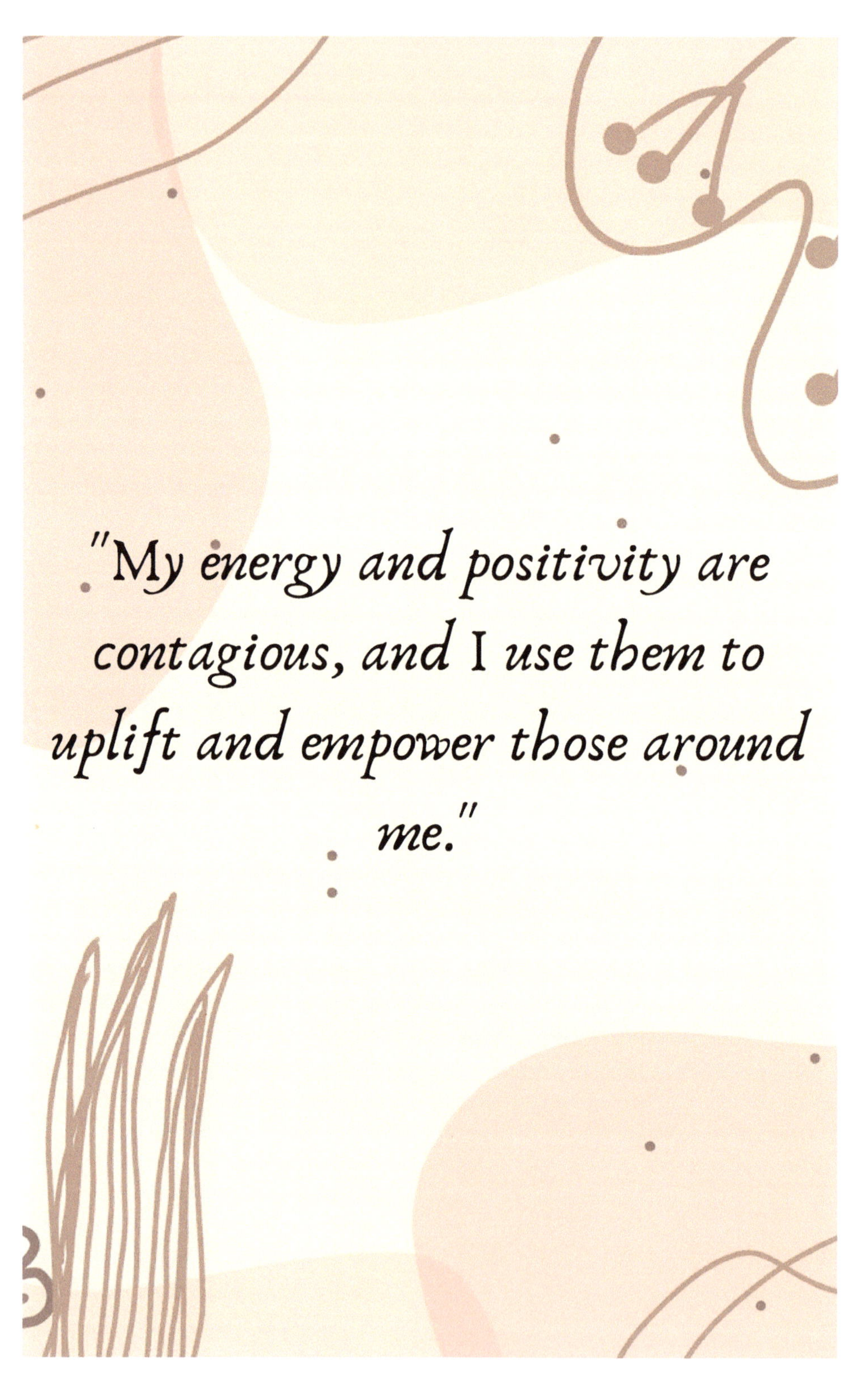

"My energy and positivity are contagious, and I use them to uplift and empower those around me."

AFFIRMATIONS

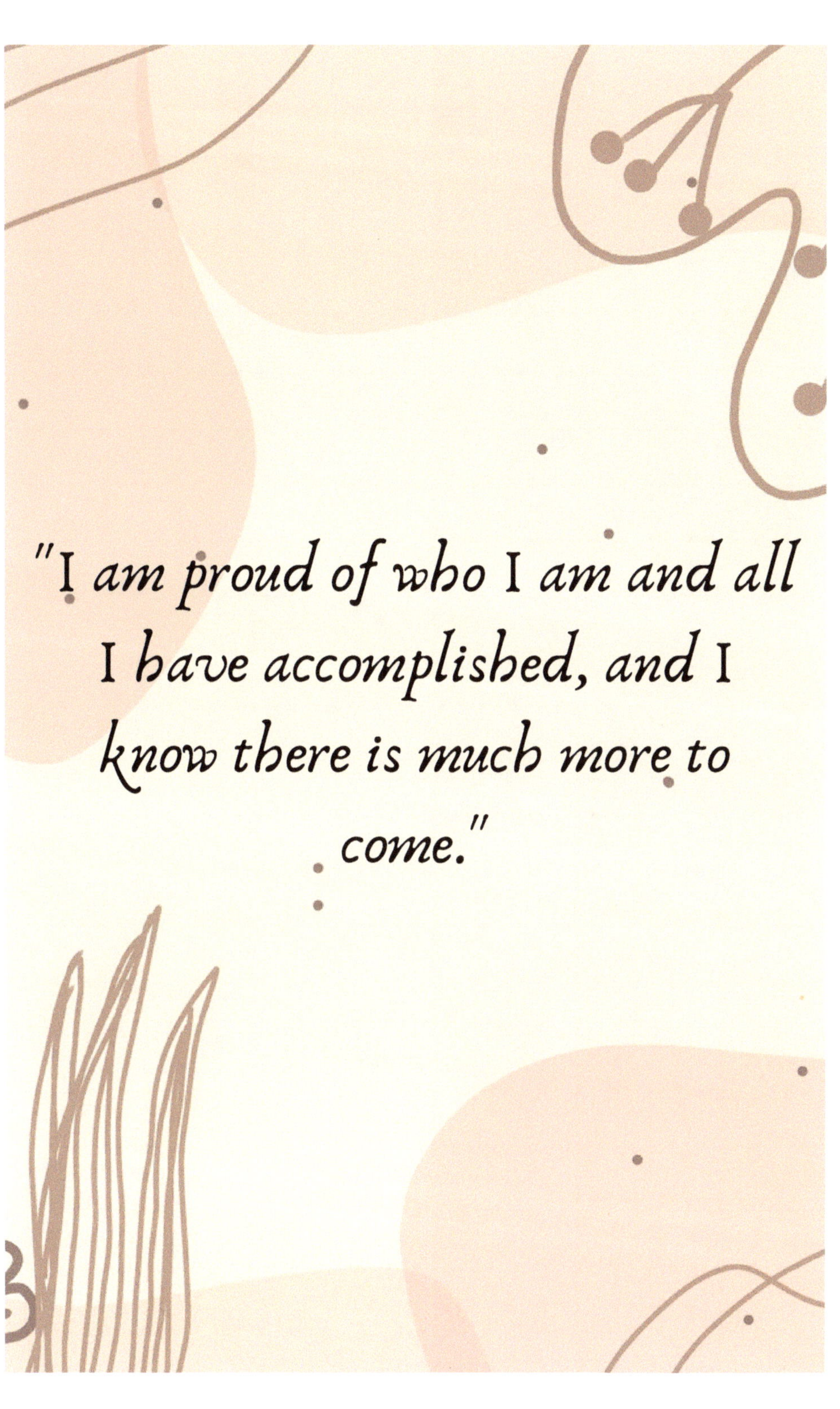

"I am proud of who I am and all I have accomplished, and I know there is much more to come."

AFFIRMATIONS

AFFIRMATIONS

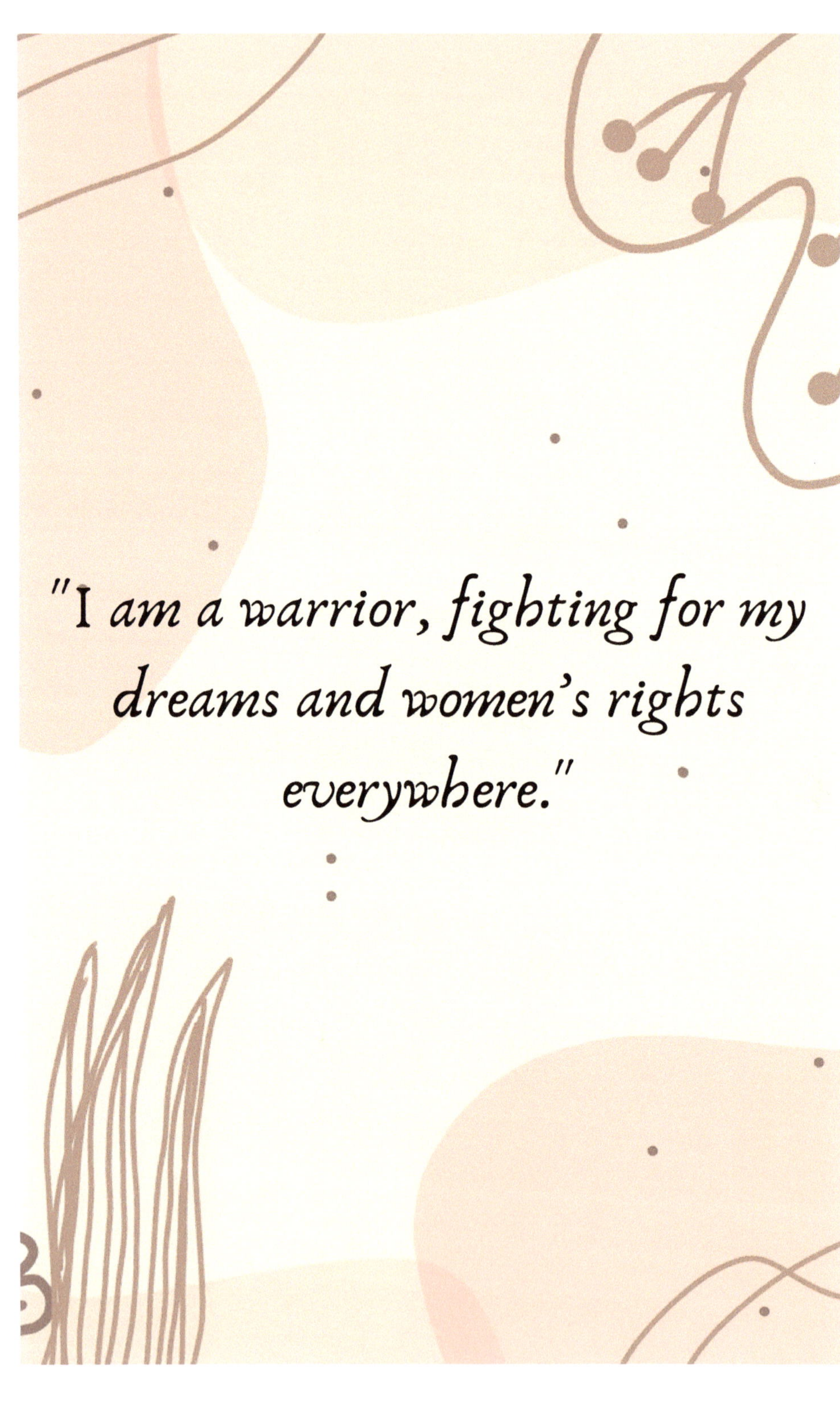

"I am a warrior, fighting for my dreams and women's rights everywhere."

AFFIRMATIONS

AFFIRMATIONS

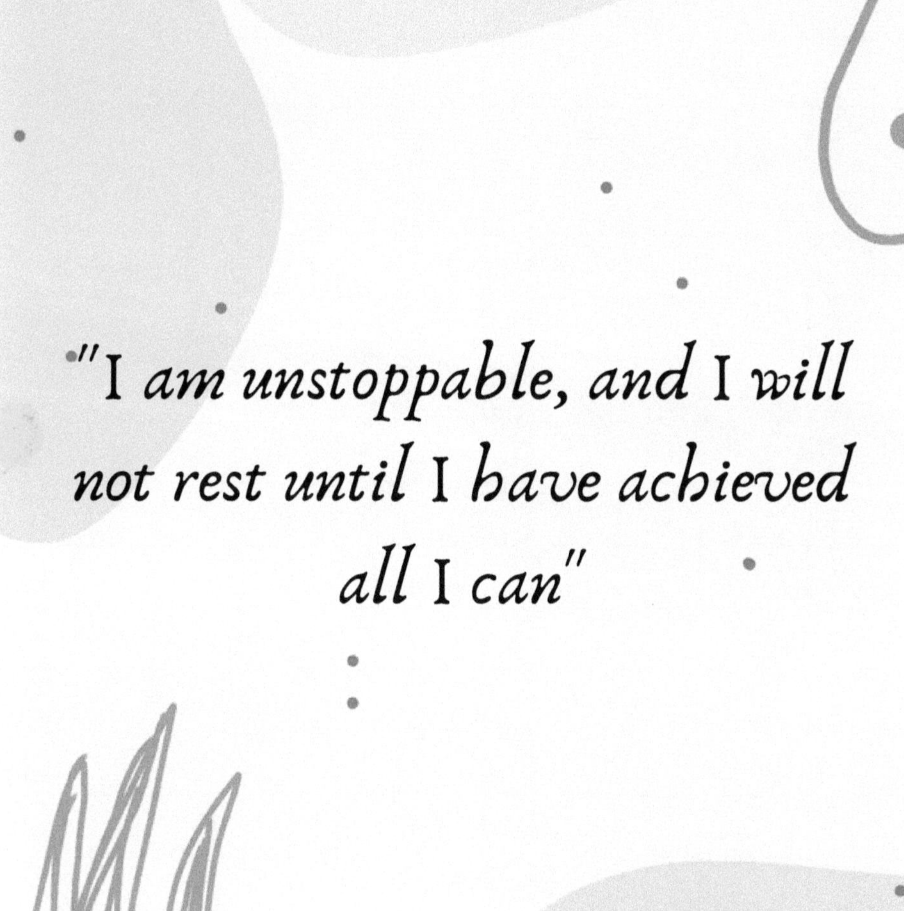
"I am unstoppable, and I will not rest until I have achieved all I can"

AFFIRMATIONS

AFFIRMATIONS

ACHIEVE MA'AM

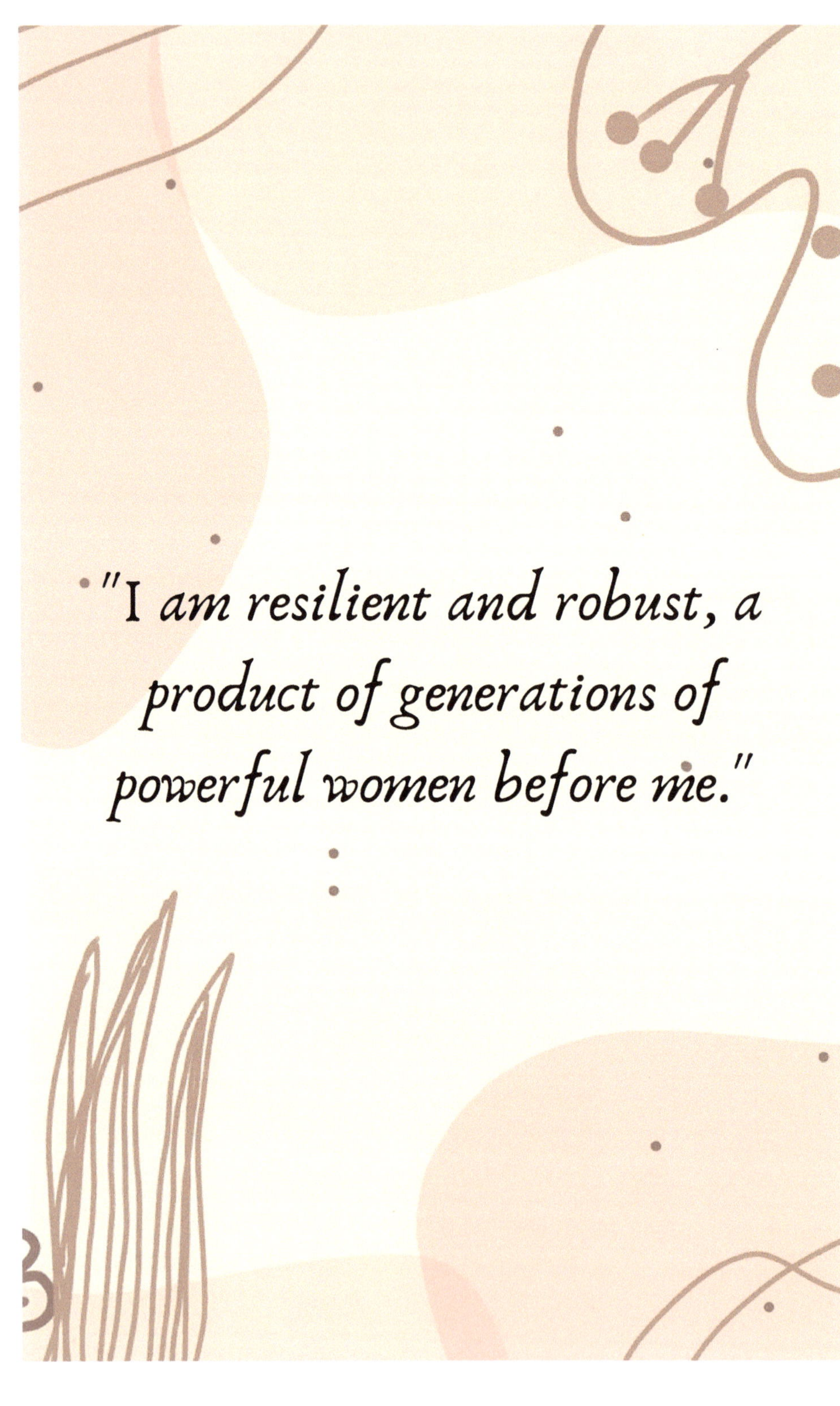
"I *am resilient and robust, a product of generations of powerful women before me.*"

AFFIRMATIONS

A

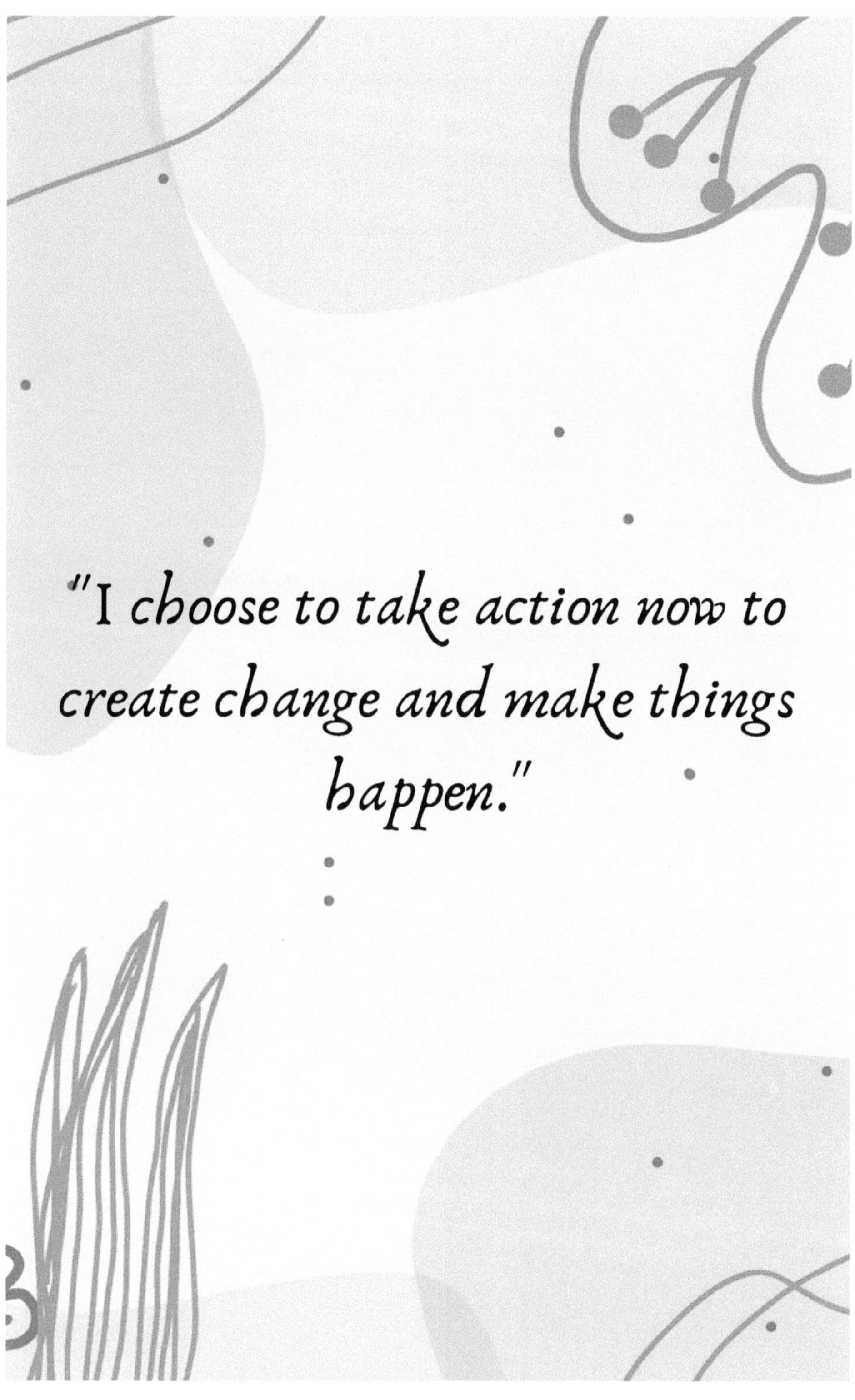
"I choose to take action now to create change and make things happen."

AFFIRMATIONS

ACHIEVE MA'AM

AFFIRMATIONS

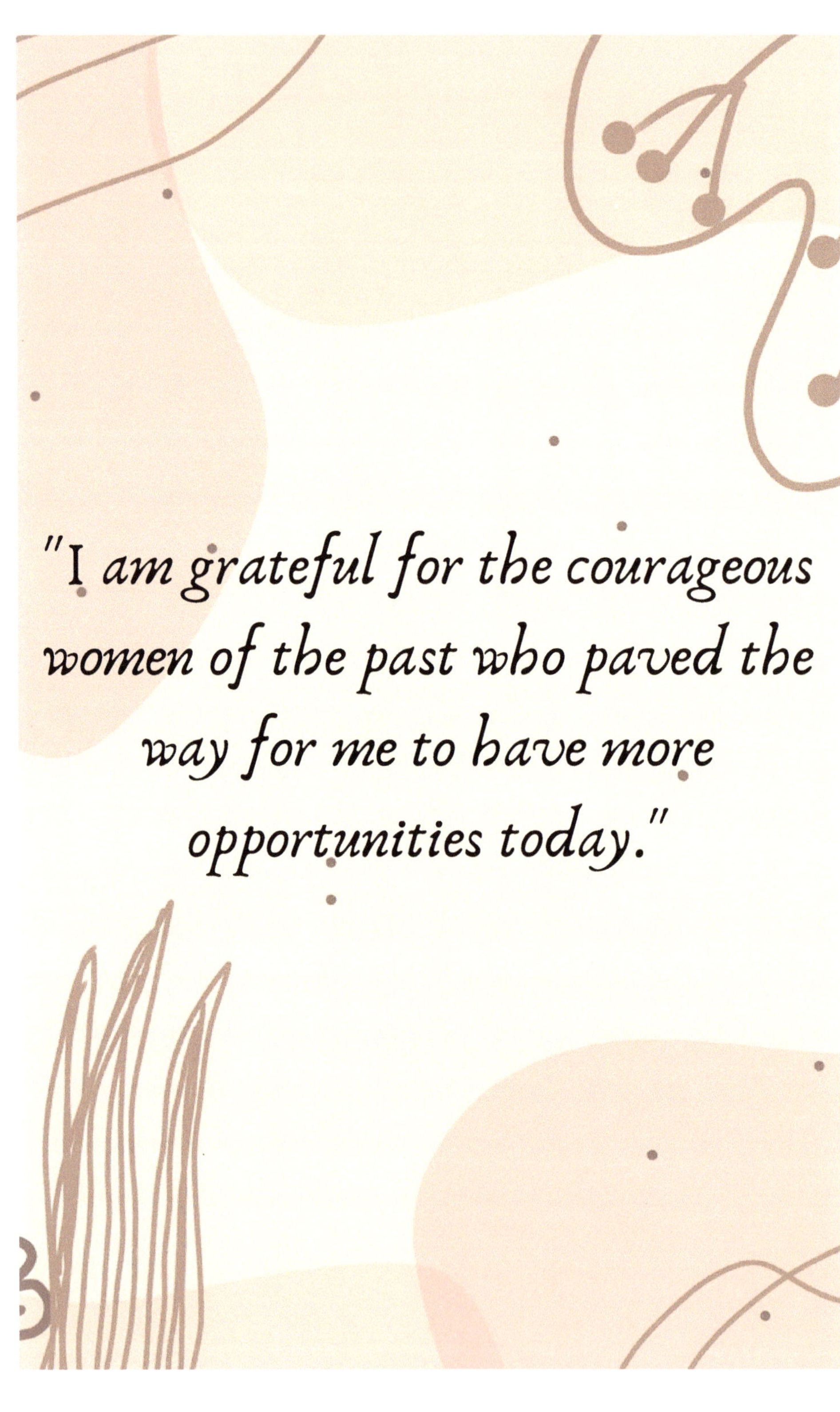

"I am grateful for the courageous women of the past who paved the way for me to have more opportunities today."

AFFIRMATIONS

AFFIRMATIONS

"I *will* not let the sting of sexism, or any other obstacle hold me back from achieving my goals."

AFFIRMATIONS

ACHIEVE MA'AM

AFFIRMATIONS

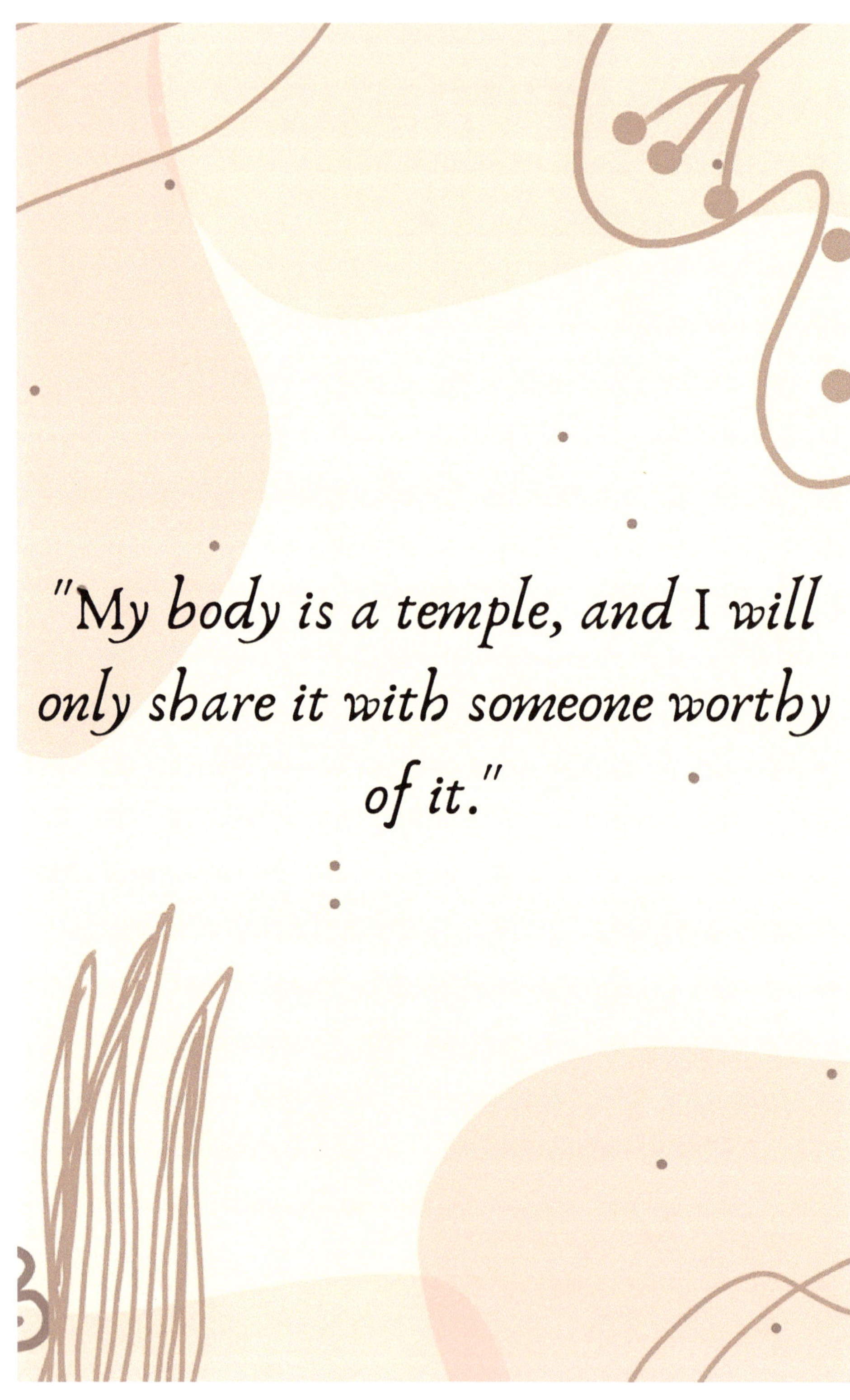
"My body is a temple, and I will only share it with someone worthy of it."

AFFIRMATIONS

AFFIRMATIONS

"I choose to surround myself with people who have overcome their fears and can support me."

AFFIRMATIONS

AFFIRMATIONS

ACHIEVE MA'AM

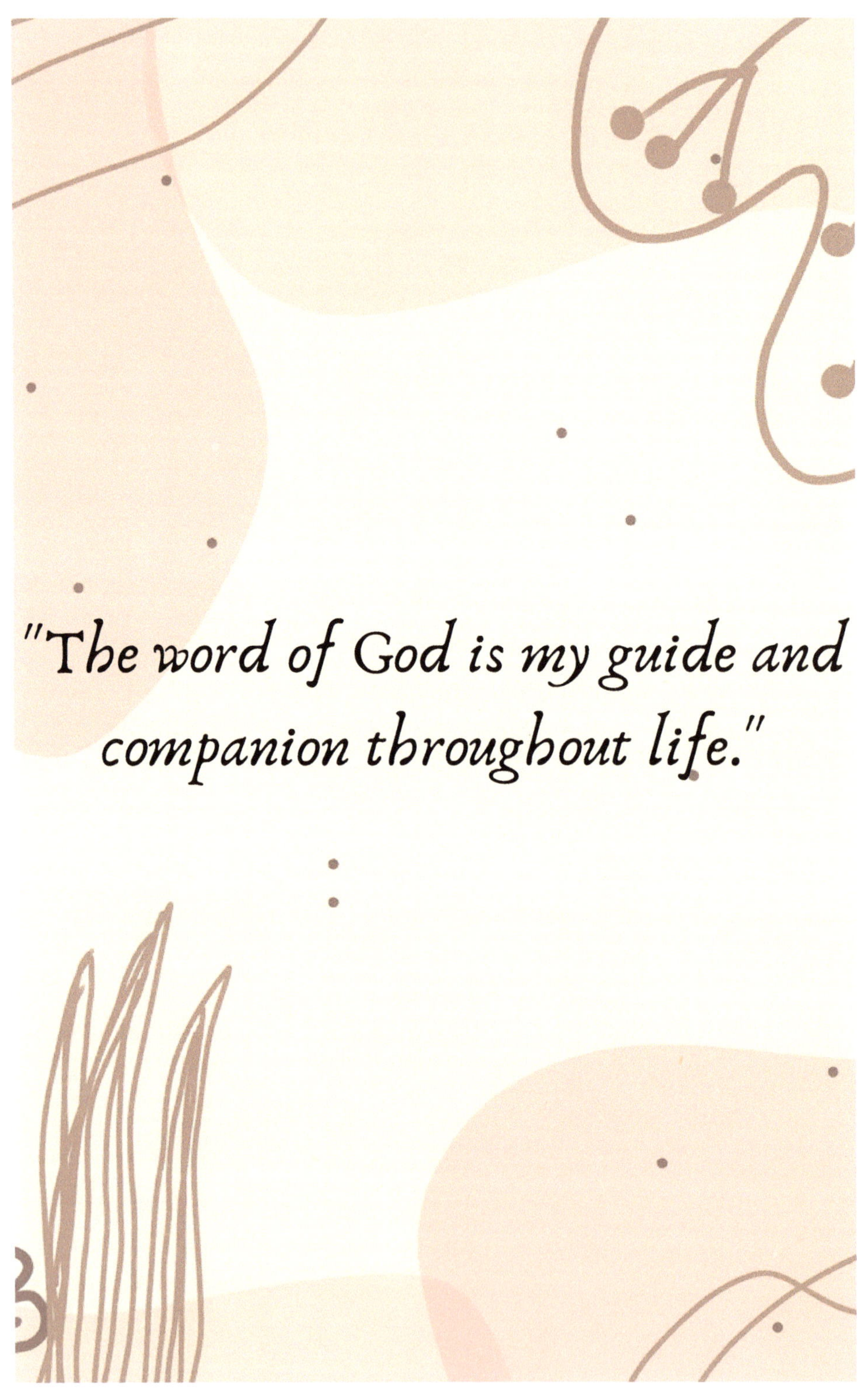
"The word of God is my guide and companion throughout life."

AFFIRMATIONS

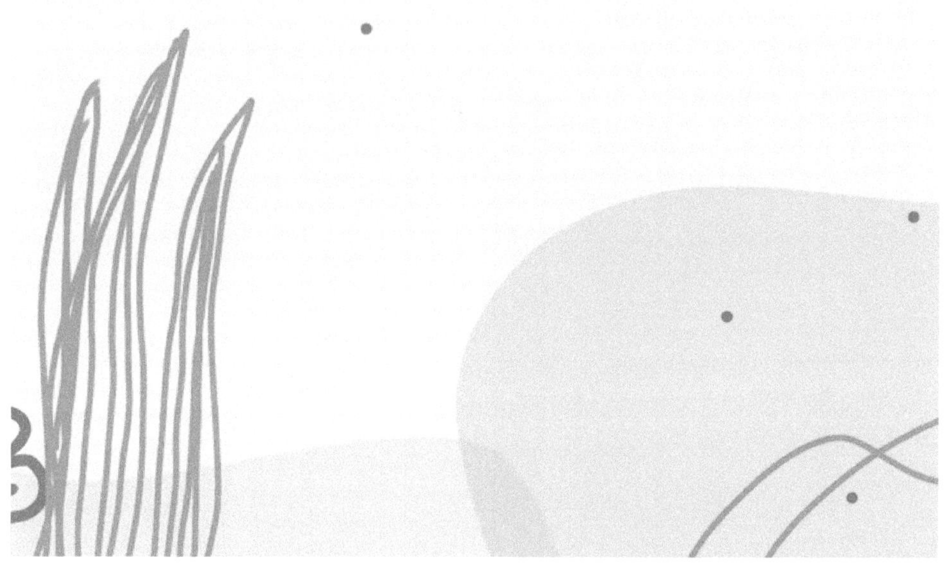

"I *am capable of being* A Proverbs 31 *woman, and* I *will act every day to become her.*"

AFFIRMATIONS

ACHIEVE MA'AM

AFFIRMATIONS

ACHIEVE MA'AM

"I can do all things through Christ who strengthens me."

AFFIRMATIONS

AFFIRMATIONS

www.ingramcontent.com/pod-product-compliance
Lightning Source LLC
Chambersburg PA
CBHW041230050726
47599CB00007B/898